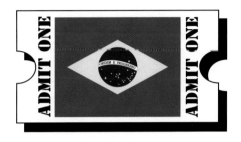

Iguazu Falls
In Southern
Brazil

FACES
AND
PLACES

# BRAZIL

BY ELMA SCHEMENAUER

THE CHILD'S WORLD®, INC.

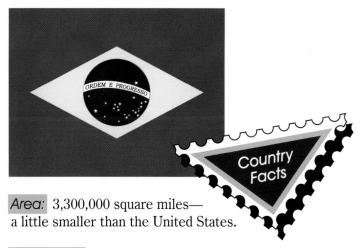

*Area:* 3,300,000 square miles—
a little smaller than the United States.

*Population:* About 164 million people.

*Capital City:* Brasília.

*Other Important Cities:* São Paulo, Rio de Janeiro, Salvador, and Belo Horizonte.

*Money:* The cruzeiro real, often called just the real (ray-AL). A real is divided into 100 centavos.

*National Flag:* A green flag with a large yellow diamond on it. Inside the yellow diamond is a blue circle of the Earth. The green stands for Brazil's rain forests. The yellow stands for the minerals that can be found in Brazil.

*National Language:* Portuguese. Spanish, English, French, and Indian languages are also spoken in Brazil.

*National Song:* "Himo Nacional Brasileiro," or "National Brazilian Hymn."

*National Holiday:* Independence Day on September 7.

*Head of Government:* The president of Brazil.

Text copyright © 2000 by The Child's World®, Inc.
All rights reserved. No part of this book may be reproduced or utilized in any form or by any means without written permission from the publisher.
Printed in the United States of America.

Library of Congress Cataloging-in-Publication Data
Schemenauer, Elma
Brazil / by Elma Schemenauer
Series: "Faces and Places".
p. cm.
Includes index.
Summary: Briefly surveys the history, geography, plants and animals, people, and culture of the largest country in South America.
ISBN 1-56766-597-7 (library : reinforced : alk. paper)

1. Brazil — Juvenile literature.
[1. Brazil] I. Title.

F2508.5.S38 1999
981 — dc21
98-46390
CIP
AC

**GRAPHIC DESIGN**
Robert A. Honey, Seattle

**PHOTO RESEARCH**
James R. Rothaus / James R. Rothaus & Associates

**ELECTRONIC PRE–PRESS PRODUCTION**
Robert E. Bonaker / Graphic Design & Consulting Co.

**PHOTOGRAPHY**
Cover photo: Samba Dancers In Costume
by Stephanie Maze/Corbis

Table
of
Contents

# Where Is Brazil?

Imagine you are on a spacecraft looking down at the planet Earth. You would see huge land areas with water around them. These land areas are called **continents**. Some continents are made up of several different countries. Brazil is a big country on the continent of South America.

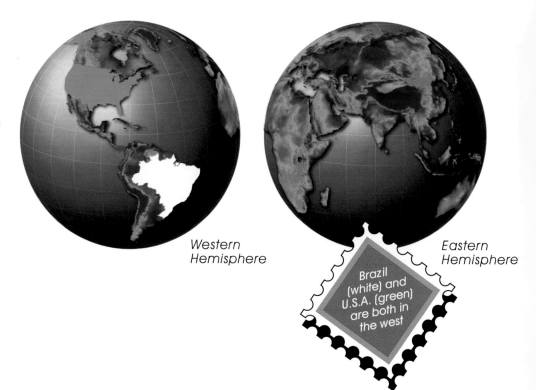

Western Hemisphere

Eastern Hemisphere

Brazil (white) and U.S.A. (green) are both in the west

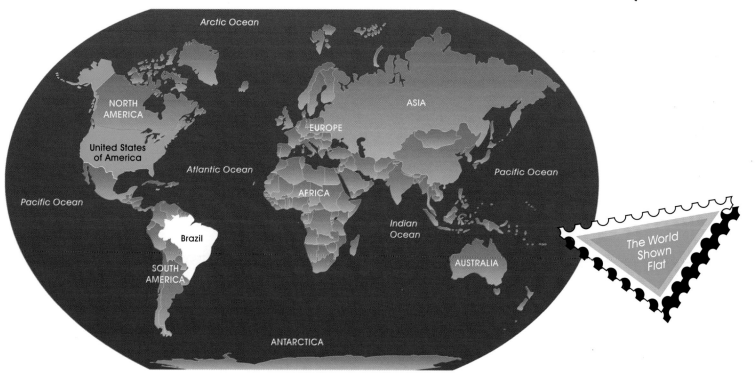

Arctic Ocean

NORTH AMERICA

United States of America

Atlantic Ocean

Pacific Ocean

EUROPE

ASIA

AFRICA

Indian Ocean

Pacific Ocean

Brazil

SOUTH AMERICA

AUSTRALIA

ANTARCTICA

The World Shown Flat

COLUMBIA

VENEZUELA   GUYANA

FRENCH GUIANA

SURINAME

Atlantic
Ocean

PERU

BRAZIL

BOLIVIA

Pacific
Ocean

PARAGUAY

CHILE

Atlantic
Ocean

ARGENTINA

URAGUAY

Amazon River

BAHIA

MATO
GROSSO

ATLANTIC
OCEAN

Aquidauana •

Iguazu Falls

Jungle On
The World's
Largest River,
The Amazon

Richard List/Corbis

Mato Grosso Marshland And Lakes

Yann Arthus-Bertrand/Corbis

**B**razil is divided into five land regions. Each area has its own kind of weather and a different type of land. The north is covered with steamy jungles. The mighty *Amazon River* runs through here, too.

The northeastern part of Brazil is hot and dry. The middle part of the country is mostly high plains. The southeastern area of Brazil has low areas and high mountains. In the country's southern parts, highlands and plains can be found.

Yann Arthus-Bertrand/Corbis

Mountain Scene Near Aquidauana

Atlantic Coast Of Bahia

Jan Butchofsky-Houser/Corbis

Brazil's huge rain forests contain millions of trees and plants. Palms, Brazil nut trees, rubber trees, and orchids all grow in the steamy weather. In the dry northeast, cactus, thorn bushes, and scrub bushes can be found. On Brazil's wide plains, thick grasslands grow in the warm sunshine.

David A. Northcott/Corbis

With so many places to live and eat, Brazil is home to lots of different kinds of animals. Monkeys, anteaters, sloths, and parrots all make their homes in the green jungles. Snakes, deer, and thousands of types of insects live there, too.

Three-Toed Sloth From Amazonas

Hyacinth Macaw From Para

Staffan Widstrand/Corbis

Squirrel Monkey From The Amazon Basin

Kevin Schafer/Corbis

Poison
Arrow
Frog

Amazon Basin

AMAZONAS    PARA

Buddy Mays/Corbis

Poison
Arrow Frog
From Northern
Brazil

Manaus

Salvador
Farol da Barra
Lighthouse

Rio de Janeiro

Colonial Buildings
In Salvador

Lighthouse Tops A Fort Built In 1598

Dave G. Houser/Corbis

**P**eople have lived in Brazil for thousands of years. The *Tupí-Guaraní* people were one of the first groups to live there. In 1500, the country of Portugal claimed Brazil as part of its kingdom. Soon Portuguese settlers came and built cities and towns. They made the native people, such as the Tupí-Guaraní, work on their farms as slaves.

In 1808, trouble in Portugal drove the Portuguese king to Brazil. He ruled there, and so did his son, *Dom Pedro*. In 1822, Dom Pedro made Brazil a country of its own. Though Brazil was no longer part of Portugal, it still had a Portuguese ruler. The ruler was in charge of making good decisions for the country.

In 1888, Brazil's slaves were set free. Some Brazilians liked this. Some did not. In the talks that followed, Brazil set up its own government.

Manaus Opera House, Built By Rubber Barons In 1896

Drawing Of The Rio de Janeiro Aquaduct, 1833

Julia Waterlow; Eye Ubiquitous/Corbis

Historical Picture Archive/Corbis

# Brazil Today

Since setting up its own government, Brazil has had different kinds of leadership. Sometimes the army has ruled by force. Sometimes the people have voted to decide who their leaders will be.

For many years Rio de Janeiro, in the Southeast region, was Brazil's capital. But since 1960, the city of Brasília has been the capital. Brasília is a modern, busy city.

Richard Bickel/Corbis

Modern Buildings In Salvador

Brazilians Celebrating Democratic Election, 1985

Stephanie Maze/Corbis

Yann Arthus-Bertrand/Corbis

Former Capital, Rio de Janeiro, And Sugarloaf Mountain

Salvador
Brasília
Rio de Janeiro

Cathedral Metropolitana In Brazília, Designed By Oscar Niemeyer

Fun And Sun Lovers Reflected In Ipanema Man's Glasses

AMAZONAS

Jericoacoara

Santo Amaro •

Ipanema Beach

# The People

ADMIT ONE — ADMIT ONE

Friends From Jericoacoara With Donkey

Many Brazilians are relatives of settlers that came over from Europe. Others are relatives of the Portuguese people. Some Brazilians are relatives of the Tupí-Guaraní people. Others are relatives of all of these groups.

The people of Brazil love to talk and smile. They also like to spend time with family and friends. Brazilians work hard at their jobs and schoolwork. They also like to have fun by celebrating lots of festivals and holidays.

Stephanie Maze/Corbis

Jan Butchofsky-Houser/Corbis

Family From Santo Amaro

Yagua Man From Amazonas Touches Botanist's Beard

Wolfgang Kaehler/Corbis

Barra Country House With A Hammock

Michael Boys/Corbis

**B**razil's cities are a lot like those in the United States. There are busy streets and tall buildings. There are hotels, shops, restaurants, and factories. There are parks and museums, too. Most city people live in apartments or small houses, just like Americans do.

In the country, many families live in stone or brick houses. Many of these have red- or orange-tiled roofs to keep out the rain. In Brazil's rain forests, where there is lots of wood, families often build wooden houses with palm-leaf roofs. Country homes often only have one or two rooms. Many country people sleep in hanging beds called **hammocks**, which they put away during the day to make more space.

Wooden 'Caboclo' Houses From Amazonas

Richard List/Corbis

Curionopolis' Row Houses Grew Up Around A Gold Site

Stephanie Maze/Corbis

AMAZONAS
Curionopolis•
Barra •
São Paulo •

Sao Paulo
Has
16,533,000
People

Yann Arthus-Bertrand/Corbis

Satiro Dias
Parana •
Pau Caboclo • • Salvador

Teenage
Student
From
Satiro Dias
Deep In
Thought

Since Brazil's weather is often hot and sticky, most Brazilian schools start at 7:00 in the morning and finish soon after lunch. Most students wear uniforms of white shirts and dark pants or skirts.

The law in Brazil says that all children must go to school until they are 14 years old. Even so, some children cannot go to school. Some live too far away. Others are too poor and must spend their days working for money to buy food. The government tries to help Brazil's children by putting lessons on radio and TV.

Girl Reading At Small School In Pau Caboclo

Stephanie Maze/Corbis

Brazil's main language is Portuguese. It sounds a bit different from what people speak in Portugal. Other languages spoken in Brazil include Spanish, English, French, and Indian languages.

Business Class For Men In Parana

Stephanie Maze/Corbis

Students Awaiting Class In Salvador

Jeremy Horner/Corbis

# Work

Because of Brazil's warm weather, many people have jobs in farming. Coffee, sugarcane, soybeans, and fruit are all grown in Brazil. Cattle and sheep are raised in many areas for their meat. Brazilians also gather nuts in the rain forest, or pick plants to make medicines.

City Brazilians have many of the same jobs that Americans do. People work in restaurants, businesses, banks, and hotels. Some work in craft shops or markets, too. Many other Brazilians work in factories. Clothes, towels, shoes, steel, ships, planes, and cars are all things that are made in Brazil.

Loading Coffee On Ships In Santos

Stephanie Maze/Corbis

Gold Mining Is Very Hard, Dirty Work, In Para

Stephanie Maze/Corbis

Welder At Volkswagen Factory In Sao Paulo

Robert Holmes/Corbis

PARA

MATO
GROSSO

São Paulo  • Santos

Stephanie Maze/Corbis

Cowboy
From The
Mato Grosso

Roasting Tapioca
In Amazonas

AMAZONAS

BAHIA

São Paulo
Mercado
Municipale

Wolfgang Kaehler/Corbis

# Food

Brazil's main foods are beans and **manioc**. Manioc is a plant root that is used to make flour. It can also be used to make tapioca for pudding. Since a lot of fruit grows in Brazil, pineapples, oranges, guavas, and other fruits are used in many dishes.

The meats Brazilians eat depend on where they live. Along the coast, people eat mostly fish. In the country, Brazilians eat beef, lamb, and pork. In some areas, people preserve meat by rubbing salt into it and hanging it in the sun to dry. This is called **sun meat**.

Produce Display In The Mercado Municipale

Robert Holmes/Corbis

Stephanie Maze/Corbis

Butcher In Small Town Market In Bahia

A Delicacy, Stuffed Piranhas For Sale In São Paulo

Robert Holmes/Corbis

**Pastimes**

Soccer, which Brazilians call *futebol*, is their favorite pastime. They play it, watch it on TV, and listen to it on the radio. They attend soccer matches in giant stadiums with thousands of other people. Another favorite Brazilian pastime is going to the beach. There people jog, surf, swim, fly kites, sunbathe, visit, and play volleyball.

Dancing To Drums On Bahia Beach

Jan Butchofsky-Houser/Corbis

Jivaro Man Plays Flute In Amazonas

Wolfgang Kaehler/Corbis

Sports Stadium In Rio de Janeiro

Yann Arthus-Bertrand/Corbis

Music is also important to Brazilians. They especially like dancing. Some of the world's most famous dances come from Brazil. They include the *bossa-nova,* the *lambada*, and the *samba*.

AMAZONAS

BAHIA

Rio de Janeiro

Copacabana
Beach

Paul Almasy/Corbis

Kites And
Vollyball At
Copacabana
Beach

Samba
Dancers
During
Carnival
In Rio de
Janeiro

RONDONIA

Salvador •

Rio de Janeiro •

# Holidays

All year long, dancing schools in the city of Rio de Janeiro practice dances for the country's biggest holiday—**Carnival**. This colorful festival happens each year in February or March. During Carnival, people dress up in bright clothes. They have huge parades and play happy music. They dance and sing happily. Other holidays in Brazil are a lot like those in the United States. Christmas and Easter are two holidays that many Brazilians celebrate each year.

Brazil is a big country with some big problems to face. In the north, mining companies and others have destroyed large areas of rain forest. This has killed many plants and animals, and is driving many people from their homes. Even though Brazilians must work hard to solve their problems, they stay happy. They are trying hard to make sure Brazil will be a strong and safe country in the future.

Big Decoration Hanging From Balcony In Salvador

Dave G. Houser/Corbis

Farmer Burning Rain Forest In Rondonia

Stephanie Maze/Corbis

Copacabana
Sidewalk In
Rio de
Janeiro

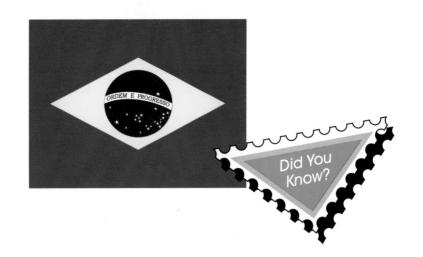

Brazil is the world's fifth largest country. Only Russia, Canada,
China, and the United States are bigger.

Brazil has more people than all the rest of South America put
together. It has the world's fifth-largest number of people.

Oil is used to make gasoline, but Brazil does not have much
oil. Some Brazilian cars run on an alcohol-based fuel made
from sugarcane or manioc.

The **equator** is an imaginary line that divides Earth in half.
Countries that lie near the equator have warm weather all
year long. The equator runs through the northern part of Brazil.
The warm, wet weather there helps thick rain forests grow.

How
Do You
Say?

| | PORTUGUESE | HOW TO SAY IT |
| --- | --- | --- |
| Hello | olá | (OH–lah) |
| Goodbye | tchau | (CHOW) |
| Please | por favor | (POR fah–VOR) |
| Thank You | obrigado | (oh–brih–GAH–doh) |
| One | um | (OOM) |
| Two | dois | (DOYSH) |
| Three | três | (TRAYZH) |
| Brazil | Brasil | (brra–ZILL) |

## Glossary

**Carnival (car–neh–VALL)**
Carnival is a Braziluan festival that is celebrated in February or March. During Carnival, people sing, dance, and have parades.

**continents (KON–tih–nents)**
Earth is divided up into land areas called continents. Brazil is on the continent of South America.

**equator (ee–KWAY–ter)**
The equator is an imaginary line that runs around the middle of Earth. Countries that lie near the equator have warm weather all year long.

**hammocks (HA–moks)**
Hammocks are beds that hang from trees or ceilings. Many country people in Brazil sleep in hammocks.

**manioc (MA–nee-ok)**
Manioc is a plant root that is crushed up and made into flour. Many Brazilian dishes are made with manioc.

**sun meat (SUN MEET)**
Sun meat is made by taking meat and rubbing salt into it. Then the meat is hung in the sunshine to dry.

## Index